Daughters of
GOD

M. RUSSELL BALLARD

DESERET
BOOK

SALT LAKE CITY, UTAH

Library of Congress Cataloging-in-Publication Data

Ballard, M. Russell, 1928–
    Daughters of God / M. Russell Ballard.
        p. cm.
    Ch. 1–2 based on addresses given by M. Russell Ballard at conferences of the Church of Jesus Christ of Latter-day Saints in April 2008 and April 1991, originally published in Ensign, May 2008, p. 108–10 and Ensign, May 1991, p. 78.
    Includes bibliographical references.
    ISBN 978-1-60641-043-1 (hardbound : alk. paper)
    1. Motherhood—Religious aspects—Church of Jesus Christ of Latter-day Saints.   2. Women—Religious aspects—Church of Jesus Christ of Latter-day Saints.   I. Title.
    BX8641.B27 2009
    248.8'431—dc22   2008046939

Printed in the United States of America
Worzalla Publishing Co., Stevens Point, WI

10   9   8   7   6   5   4   3   2   1

CONTENTS

Photo credits: p. xiv, Jerzyworks/Masterfile/Getty Images; p. 5, Emin Kuliyev/Shutterstock; p. 8, Steve Wisbauer/Digital Vision/Getty Images; p. 16, Kim Winderman/fstop/Getty Images; p. 21, Aleksandar Milosevic/Shutterstock; p. 26, Rob Marmion/Shutterstock; p. 36, Birute Vijeikiene/Shutterstock; p. 41, Maja Schon/Shutterstock; p. 46, Getty Images; p. 51, Saniphoto/Shutterstock; p. 56, Kenneth Sponsler/Shutterstock.

FOREWORD

The women of The Church of Jesus Christ of Latter-day Saints may have no more enthusiastic fan—on earth, that is—than Elder M. Russell Ballard of the Quorum of the Twelve. This is at least partly because of the influence of his wife, Barbara, who is the joy of his life and who, by his own admission, has taught him a thing or two during their fifty-seven years of marriage. Anything she might have missed, his five daughters, twenty-four granddaughters, and nine great-granddaughters have filled in—again by his own admission. Which is why he has suggested, on several occasions, that his practical, on-the-job training has made him an expert on women.

I might state it just a bit differently. From my experience, Elder Ballard is without question an expert on not only understanding but also appreciating the strength, the resilience, the vision, and the influence of righteous, latter-day women of God. He expressed the scope of his admiration in an address at the 2003 BYU Women's Conference, where he stated, "We are now thirteen million strong in this Church, but we have so much more work to do. Let us never, ever forget that this work is all about people. It is about boys and girls, young men and young women, men and women, and families. And—dare I say it?—*no one has more influence over boys and girls, young men and young women, men and women, and the families of the Church and even of the world than do you, my sisters, whose influence because of your mothering and mentoring nature is unparalleled.* Never, ever make the mistake of underestimating the influence of women. There are few things as powerful, as nurturing, or as life-changing as the influence of a righteous woman" (emphasis added).

As affirming as those words are—and Elder Ballard has spoken similarly in countless settings through the years—from both observation and personal experience, I can say that Elder Ballard not only talks the talk, but he walks the walk.

For twenty-five years or so, I have had the privilege of learning from Elder Ballard in a variety of settings. He served as chairman of the board of Deseret Book Company for a season when I worked as an officer of that company. Some years ago he was serving as executive director of the Missionary Department when I was called upon to help with a project there. He presided over the

Priesthood Executive Committee while I served as a counselor in the Relief Society general presidency, which fell under PEC direction. And there have been numerous other projects through the years when I have worked under his direction and benefited from his leadership, his savvy, and his sage counsel. Again and again, I have both experienced and observed the seemingly natural but profound respect he has for us as women—for our judgment, our insight, our ability to contribute to councils in meaningful and important ways, our propensity for working past the point of exhaustion in the service of others, and our unique gifts and the expression of them.

Elder Ballard has spoken again and again, including in general conference, on the importance of councils—in both the Church and the family— and the strength that comes when righteous men and righteous women combine their efforts in the service of the Lord. More than once, as I reported back to Elder Ballard on one assignment or another, and particularly those that called for deliberation, I found myself wondering if I wasn't experiencing an ideal pattern. He welcomes candid expression, listens, considers what he hears, then counsels. Never while serving or working under his direction have I heard so much as a patronizing syllable, never a hint of dismissiveness, never anything other than an almost effortless inclusiveness that acknowledges how unique and necessary our voices are and how vital our ability to love and nurture is to boys and girls, young men and young women, husbands and loved ones, and, without sounding unduly hyperbolic, all mankind.

It is for this reason that the publishing division of Deseret Book approached Elder Ballard about compiling in this small gift book three of his classic messages—"Daughters of God," "Teach the

Children," and "As Women of God"—that reinforce his deep feelings about the importance of mothers, motherhood, and womanhood itself. These teachings from a prophet, seer, and revelator who has such obvious regard for the divine nature of women are reassuring, encouraging, motivating, and filled with meaning for every woman. They bear reading and pondering again and again.

"I hope all of you dear sisters, married or single, never wonder if you have worth in the sight of the Lord and to the leaders of the Church," he said at the conclusion of "Daughters of God." "We love you. We respect you and appreciate your influence in preserving the family and assisting with the growth and the spiritual vitality of the Church. . . . I pray that God will continually bless the women of the Church to find joy and happiness in their sacred roles as daughters of God."

May every woman who reads, studies, and

ponders Elder Ballard's words come to know for herself that what he teaches about all of us is true for every one of us.

—Sheri Dew

DAUGHTERS OF GOD

The year my wife, Barbara, had back surgery and could not lift, twist, or bend, I did more lifting, twisting, and bending than ever before. It made me more appreciative of what women, and especially mothers, do every day in our homes.

While women live in homes under many different circumstances—married, single, widowed, or divorced, some with children and some without—all are beloved of God, and He has a plan for His righteous daughters to receive the highest blessings of eternity.

As a young father, I learned the demanding role of motherhood. I served as a counselor in a bishopric and then as bishop for a period of ten years. During that time we were blessed with six of our seven children. Barbara was often worn out by the time I got home Sunday evening. She tried to explain what it was like to sit on the back row in sacrament meeting with our young family.

Then the day came that I was released. After sitting on the stand for ten years, I was now sitting with my family on the back row.

The ward's singing mothers' chorus was providing the music one Sunday, and I found myself sitting alone with our six children. I have never been so busy in my whole life. I had the hand puppets going on both hands, and that wasn't working too well. The Cheerios got away from me, and that was embarrassing. The coloring books didn't seem to entertain as well as they should.

As I struggled with the children through the meeting, I looked up at Barbara, and she was watching me and smiling. I learned for myself to more fully appreciate what mothers do so well and so faithfully!

A generation later, as a grandfather, I have watched the sacrifices my daughters have made in rearing their children. And now, still another generation later, I am watching with awe the pressures on my granddaughters as they guide their children in this busy and demanding world.

After observing and empathizing with three generations of mothers and thinking of my own dear mother, I surely know that there is no role in life more essential and more eternal than that of motherhood.

There is no one perfect way to be a good

mother. Each situation is unique. Each mother has different challenges, different skills and abilities, and certainly different children. The choice is different and unique for each mother and each family. Many are able to be "full-time moms," at least during the most formative years of their children's lives, and many others would like to be. Some may have to work part- or full-time; some may work at home; some may divide their lives into periods of home and family and work. What matters is that a mother loves her children deeply and, in keeping with the devotion she has for God and her husband, prioritizes them above all else.

I am impressed by countless mothers who have learned how important it is to focus on the things that can be done only in a particular season of life. If a child lives with parents for eighteen or nineteen years, that span is only one-fourth of a parent's life. And the most formative time of all, the

early years in a child's life, represent less than one-tenth of a parent's normal life. It is crucial to focus on our children for the short time we have them with us and to seek, with the help of the Lord, to teach them all we can before they leave our homes. This eternally important work falls to mothers and fathers as equal partners. I am grateful that today many fathers are more involved in the lives of their children. But I believe that the instincts and the intense, nurturing involvement of mothers with their children will always be a major key to those children's well-being. In the words of the proclamation on the family, "Mothers are primarily responsible for the nurture of their children" ("The Family: A Proclamation to the World," *Ensign,* November 1995, 102).

We need to remember that the full commitment of motherhood and of putting children first can be difficult. Through my own four-generation experience in our family, and through discussions with mothers of young children throughout the Church, I know something of a mother's emotions that accompany her commitment to be at home with young children. There are moments of great joy and incredible fulfillment, but there are also moments of a sense of inadequacy, monotony, and frustration. Mothers may feel they receive little or no appreciation for the choice they have made. Sometimes even husbands seem to have no idea of the demands upon their wives.

As a Church, we have enormous respect and gratitude to you mothers of young children. We want you to be happy and successful in your families and to have the validation and support you need and deserve. So let me ask and briefly answer four questions. While my answers may seem extremely simple, if the simple things are being tended to, a mother's life can be most rewarding.

The first question: What can you do, as a young mother, to reduce the pressure and enjoy your family more?

First, recognize that the joy of motherhood comes in moments. There will be hard times and frustrating times. But amid the challenges, there are shining moments of joy and satisfaction.

Author Anna Quindlen reminds us not to rush past the fleeting moments. She said: "The biggest mistake I made [as a parent] is the one that most of us make. . . . I did not live in the moment enough. This is particularly clear now that the moment is gone, captured only in photographs. There is one picture of [my three children] sitting in the grass on a quilt in the shadow of the swing set on a summer day, ages six, four, and one. And I wish I could remember what we ate, and what we talked about, and how they sounded, and how they looked when they slept that night. I wish I had not been in such a hurry to get on to the next thing: dinner, bath, book, bed. I wish I had treasured the doing a little more and the getting it done a little less" (*Loud and Clear* [Random House, 2004], 10–11).

Second, don't overschedule yourselves or your children. We live in a world that is filled with options. If we are not careful, we will find every minute jammed with social events, classes, exercise time, book clubs, scrapbooking, Church callings, music, sports, the Internet, and our favorite TV shows. One mother told me of a time when her children had twenty-nine scheduled commitments every week: music lessons, Scouts, dance, Little League, day camps, soccer, art, and so forth. She felt like a taxi driver. Finally, she called a family meeting and announced, "Something has to go; we have no time to ourselves and no time for each other." Families need unstructured time in which relationships can deepen and real parenting can take place. Take time to listen, to laugh, and to play together.

Third, even as you try to cut out the extra commitments, find some time for yourself to cultivate your gifts and interests. Pick one or two things that you would like to learn or do that will enrich your life, and make time for them. Water cannot be drawn from an empty well, and if you are not setting aside a little time for what replenishes you, you will have less and less to give to others, even to your children. Avoid any kind of substance abuse, mistakenly thinking that it will help you accomplish more. And don't allow yourself to be caught up in the time-wasting, mind-numbing things like television soap operas or surfing the Internet. Turn to the Lord in faith, and you will know what to do and how to do it.

Fourth, pray, study, and teach the gospel. Pray

deeply about your children and about your role as a mother. Parents can offer a unique and wonderful kind of prayer because they are praying to the Eternal Parent of us all. There is great power in a prayer that essentially says, "We are steward-parents over Thy children, Father; please help us to raise them as Thou wouldst want them raised."

The second question: What more can a husband do to support his wife, the mother of their children?

First, show extra appreciation and give more validation for what your wife does every day. Notice things and say thank you—often. Schedule some evenings together, just the two of you.

Second, have a regular time to talk with your wife about each child's needs and what you can do to help.

Third, give your wife a "day away" now and then. Just take over the household and give your wife a break from her daily responsibilities. Taking over for a while will greatly enhance your appreciation of what your wife does. You may do a lot of lifting, twisting, and bending!

Fourth, come home from work and take an active role with your family. Don't put work, friends, or sports ahead of listening to, playing with, and teaching your children.

The third question: What can children, even young children, do? You may wish to sit your children down and share these ideas with them:

There are some simple things you can do to help your mother.

You can pick up your toys when you are finished playing with them, and when you get a little older, you can make your bed, help with the dishes, and do other chores—without being asked.

You can say thank you more often when you finish a nice meal, when a story is read to you at bedtime, or when clean clothes are put in your drawers.

Most of all, you can put your arms around your mother often and tell her you love her.

The last question: What can the Church do?

There are many things the Church offers to mothers and families, but may I suggest here that the bishopric and the ward council members be especially watchful and considerate of the time and resource demands on young mothers and their families. Know them and be wise in what you ask them to do at this time in their lives. Alma's counsel to his son Helaman applies to us today: "Behold I say unto you, that by small and simple things are great things brought to pass" (Alma 37:6).

I hope that all of you dear sisters, married or single, never wonder if you have worth in the sight of the Lord and to the leaders of the Church. We love you. We respect you and appreciate your influence in preserving the family and assisting with the growth and the spiritual vitality of the Church. Let us remember that "the family is central to the Creator's plan for the eternal destiny of His children" ("The Family: A Proclamation to the World"). The scriptures and the teachings of the prophets and apostles help all family members to prepare together now to be together through all eternity. I pray that God will continually bless the women of the Church to find joy and happiness in their sacred roles as daughters of God.

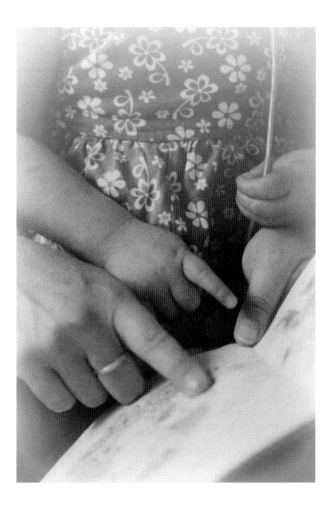

TEACH THE CHILDREN

One year, I had the privilege of participating in the Washington, D.C., Visitors' Center Christmas lighting celebration. When I turned on the 200,000 lights, they seemed to dance and sparkle in the trees, with the majestic temple glowing in the background. That night, outside of their Soviet community for the first time, thirty-five children from the Soviet Embassy School performed. They presented beautifully the dances and songs of their homeland. Following their program, boys and girls who were members of the

Church performed for an appreciative audience that included embassy officials from twenty-two nations.

The children who were members of the Church were sitting on risers that had been placed directly in front of the eight-foot *Christus* statue that stands as the focal point of the visitors' center lobby. The Soviet children were sitting with their teachers and parents apart from our youngsters. When I stood to speak, these beautiful young people with their vibrant countenances captured my attention. I asked the Soviet boys and girls to come and sit with our youth. As they did, it was a beautiful sight and an appropriate way to begin the Christmas season. Sweet and pure children from two powerful nations showed an instant love for one another as they were seated at the feet of the *Christus.*

I said to the audience that perhaps the world's troubles could be solved if we could turn over the leadership of nations to the children for a few days. Through love they would find solutions to the misunderstandings, mistrust, and misconduct of adults in the world. I had the clear impression that night that if all men and women could love Jesus Christ as these lovely children do, many world problems could be solved. Sooner, perhaps, than we realize, the fate of nations will be in the hands of today's children. An anonymous author penned it this way:

I saw tomorrow passing on little children's feet
And on their forms and faces her prophecies
* complete.*
And then I saw tomorrow look at me through
* little children's eyes.*
And I thought how carefully I must teach if I
* am wise!*

If we are concerned about our tomorrows, we will teach our children wisely and carefully, for in them lie our tomorrows.

Have you seen the future when you gazed through the hospital nursery window and saw the bassinet wheeled into your view? You see that beautiful newborn infant for the first time. A new spirit comes into your life as a son or daughter, grandchild, or child of a friend, and you know that your life will never be quite the same again. How often have you had to blink back the tears as you stood in awe and contemplated the miracle of a new life? This newly arrived spirit has come in sweet innocence from the presence of God.

Every human being is a spirit child of God and lived with Heavenly Father before coming to earth. He entrusts His spirit children to earthly parents who provide a mortal body for them through the miracle of physical birth and gives to parents the sacred opportunity and responsibility to love, protect, teach, and bring them up in light and truth so they may one day, through the Atonement and

Resurrection of Jesus Christ, return to our Father's presence.

These precious souls come to us in purity and innocence. As parents, we assume an immense responsibility for their care and well-being. Parents share this sacred trust with brothers and sisters, grandparents, teachers, neighbors, and all who touch the lives and impress or influence the souls of these precious children. King Benjamin admonished parents many years ago, "But ye will teach them to walk in the ways of truth and soberness; ye will teach them to love one another, and to serve one another" (Mosiah 4:15).

The critical nature of the first tender formative years cannot be overstated. These little ones are like seedlings in a plant nursery. All look much the same in the beginning, but each one will grow to become independent and unique. Parents are to nourish, tend, and teach their children so they will grow to their full stature and potential.

Parents and teachers should see beyond the little girl in pigtails and should not be misled by the ragged little boy with a dirty face and holes in the knees of his pants. True teachers and leaders see children as they may become. They see the valiant missionary who will one day share his testimony with the world and later become a righteous father who honors his priesthood. The inspired teacher sees pure and beautiful mothers and future presidents of the Relief Society, Young Women, and Primary, even though today they may be girls who giggle and chatter on the back row in the classroom. Sometimes people say, "Well, boys will be boys!" Not so—boys will be men, and almost before we know it.

To see our children grow, succeed, and take their places in society and in the Lord's kingdom is an eternal reward worth any inconvenience or sacrifice.

Oh, that every parent could understand that children come from a premortal experience and have possibilities that often are far beyond what we might expect. We should spare no effort to help our children reach their full potential. Is it any wonder that Jesus brought the little children unto himself to teach and bless them? He said, "Whosoever shall receive one of such children in my name, receiveth me" (Mark 9:37). He also said, "Even so it is not the will of your Father which is in heaven, that one of these little ones should perish" (Matthew 18:14).

When asked, "Who is the greatest in the kingdom of heaven?" the Savior "called a little child unto him, and set him in the midst of them, and said, Verily I say unto you, Except ye be converted, and become as little children, ye shall not enter into the kingdom of heaven. Whosoever therefore shall humble himself as this little child, the same is greatest in the kingdom of heaven" (Matthew 18:1–4).

A recent experience illustrates the importance of each of these little children. One Saturday morning I was preparing for an activity with one of my grandsons. But before we could make our exit out the door, I heard another small voice inquiring, "Can I go too, Grandpa?" Did you ever try to say no to such a request? That activity would not have been the same without that someone else who really wanted to "go too." Just as surely, heaven will not be heaven if some of our children who want to "go too" are left behind.

Some may choose not to go. Our Heavenly Father has given them the agency to choose for themselves. We have the task of helping them learn about our Heavenly Father's plan for us, demonstrating our faith in the Lord, and continuing to

work with our children in prayerful and patient persuasion.

If we are to teach our children the gospel of Jesus Christ and to protect them from the influences of a wicked world, love must abide in our homes. We should cherish and care for our children with unwavering dedication. The older we grow, the more precious our family becomes to us. We come to see more clearly that all of the wealth, honor, and positions of the world pale in significance when compared to the precious souls of our loved ones. You young parents who are beginning your families must guard against seeking financial gain, worldly comforts, or achievement at the expense of your children. You must guard against being so anxious to get to work or to a meeting that you do not have time for your family, especially time to listen to anxious little voices. Always remember this timeless counsel from a prophet of

God, President David O. McKay: "No other success can compensate for failure in the home" ("The Editor's Page," *Improvement Era,* June 1964, 445).

We cannot and we must not allow the school, community, television, or even Church organizations to establish our children's values. The Lord has placed this duty with mothers and fathers. It is one from which we cannot escape and one that cannot be delegated. Others may help, but parents remain accountable. Therefore, we must guard the sanctity of our homes because that is where children develop their values, attitudes, and habits for everyday living.

Children perceive their own identity much earlier than we may realize. They want to be recognized as individuals. Not long ago, as my wife visited with our daughter, her three-year-old son ran to his grandmother. She picked him up and said, "Hi, how are you doing, Babes?" He looked at her and said with a serious voice, "I not a Babes, I a Dude!" In the vernacular of the day, he was asserting that he was someone special, he had a place, and he belonged.

What a beautiful place this world will be when all parents, fathers and mothers, see the importance of teaching their children the principles that will help them be happy and successful. Parents teach best when they lead by good example; govern their little ones with patience, kindness, and love unfeigned; and have the same spirit of love for children that Jesus exemplified.

In times of need, a father may bless his children through the righteous exercise of his priesthood. Every mother can accept her children from her Father in Heaven as her great source of joy. She will know that because her children are also children of God, no sacrifice is too great to protect them from evil and to surround them with a spirit of love and trust in God.

One of our grandsons, when he was five years old, became confused when his family moved into a new ward. He thought the meetings were over and went outside. When he realized he was alone and could not find the family or their car, he knelt down and prayed for help. Just a few minutes later, one of the counselors in the Primary presidency came out and asked him if he was lost. A Primary teacher had called to her from the door of a classroom and said that someone was missing. The teacher asked the counselor to find out who it was. The counselor felt impressed to look outside and went straight to our grandson. Later, the teacher and counselor both commented on how strong their impressions were that he needed help. We were thankful that his parents and Primary teachers had taught him that Heavenly Father loves him and had taught him to always pray for help.

Priesthood leaders should select dedicated, spiritually guided Primary teachers. Teachers should teach by love and example after prayerful preparation. A loving teacher each Sunday can calm the fear of new surroundings and help children want to come to Church meetings. One five-year-old girl began to cry as the family was preparing for Sunday meetings. When asked why, she sobbed, "I don't know who my teacher will be." Her class had had several teachers in recent months; the frequent change had disturbed the peace of that tender little soul.

Our children do not grow to full physical stature suddenly. In like manner, their spiritual growth takes place over time. This development might be compared to erecting a block building. The walls are formed block by block, with a strong mortar holding each block to the others. We could give these building blocks names, such as bedtime stories, listening to a child pray, tucking a child in bed at night, and a quiet review of the day's activities. Other blocks could be pleasant dinner conversations, praise for tasks well done, birthday parties, and family outings. Others could be doing your chores, being kind to one another, reading from the scriptures together, serving others, and saying I love you. Still other blocks could be learning to work, taking responsibility, respecting elders, singing together, doing homework, attending Primary, and honoring the Sabbath day. Even larger blocks are family home evening, respecting and honoring the priesthood, and family prayer.

A vast array of such beautiful building blocks that are placed carefully can form a fortress of faith that the tidal waves of worldly distraction and evil cannot breach. These blocks are held together with a mortar called love: love of Heavenly Father and his Son Jesus Christ, love of parents, love for each other, love for choosing the good.

Many children have only one parent at home, and some are left with no parents at all. We all share a responsibility to help fill such voids and to provide sustained assistance and encouragement.

On the negative side, we hear disturbing reports of parents or guardians who are so far removed from the Spirit of Christ that they abuse children. Whether this abuse is physical, verbal, or the less evident but equally severe emotional abuse, it is an abomination and a serious offense to God. Jesus left no question about the seriousness of harming children in any way when he said, "But whoso shall offend one of these little ones which believe in me, it were better for him that a millstone were hanged about his neck, and that he were drowned in the depth of the sea" (Matthew 18:6).

We plead with you to take time for your children and your grandchildren while they are young. Special moments may come only once. Before we are aware, they have grown older, and our best opportunity for teaching them how to live happy and fulfilling lives is past.

I know that we are all spirit children of a loving Heavenly Father, every one of us with a glorious destiny, if we will humble ourselves as little children and keep the commandments of God. May we be blessed with the Spirit of Christ in our own lives, and may we have his Spirit with us in teaching little children.

AS WOMEN OF GOD

I once received an outline called "A Woman's Lifeline" that I can relate to because I've seen a number of little girls grow up, and I thought you might be able to relate to it also.

Age 3: She looks at herself and sees a queen.

Age 8: She looks at herself and sees Cinderella.

Age 15: She looks at herself and sees an ugly duckling. ("Mom, I can't go to school looking like this today!")

Age 20: She looks at herself and sees "too fat/too thin, too short/too tall, too straight/too curly" but decides she's going out anyway.

Age 30: She looks at herself and sees "too fat/too thin, too short/too tall, too straight/too curly" but decides she doesn't have time to fix it so she's going out anyway.

Age 40: She looks at herself and sees "too fat/too thin, too short/too tall, too straight/too curly" but says, "At least I am clean," and goes out anyway.

Age 50: She looks at herself and sees "I am what I am" and goes wherever she wants to go.

Age 60: She looks at herself and reminds herself of all the people who can't even see themselves in the mirror anymore. Goes out and conquers the world.

Age 70: She looks at herself and sees wisdom, laughter, and ability and goes out and enjoys life.

Age 80: Doesn't bother to look. Just puts on a purple hat and goes out to have fun with the world.

The moral is, maybe we should all grab that purple hat a little earlier.

The reason I am concerned about you dear women of the Church, knowing how important you are to the Lord, is expressed in a letter I have in my possession that came to us at the Church offices. A good sister wrote:

"I have a wonderful husband and children, whom I love deeply. I love the Lord and His Church more than I can say. I know the Church is true! I realize I shouldn't feel discouraged about who I am. Yet I have been going through an identity crisis most of my life. I have never dared utter these feelings out loud but have hidden them behind the huge, confident smile I wear to Church every week.

"For years I have doubted if I had any value beyond my roles as a wife and mother. I have feared that men are that they might have joy but women are that they might be overlooked. I long to feel that I as a woman matter to the Lord."

If you have ever wondered, "Does the Lord respect women? Do women matter to the Lord? Do women matter to the leaders of the Church?" the answer is a resounding YES!

Elder James E. Talmage stated that "the world's greatest champion of woman and womanhood is Jesus the Christ" (*Jesus the Christ* [Deseret Book, 1983], 441). I believe that is a true statement. The first time the Lord acknowledged Himself to be the

Christ was to a Samaritan woman at Jacob's well. He taught her about living water and proclaimed, simply, "I . . . am he" (John 4:26). And it was Martha to whom He proclaimed, "I am the resurrection, and the life . . . And whosoever liveth and believeth in me shall never die" (John 11:25–26).

And then, during His greatest agony as He hung on the cross, the Savior reached out to one person, His mother. In that terrible but glorious moment He asked John the Beloved to care for her as though she were his own (see John 19:26–27).

Of this you may be certain: The Lord especially loves righteous women—women who are not only faithful but filled with faith, women who are optimistic and cheerful because they know who they are and where they are going, women who are striving to live and serve as women of God.

There are those who suggest that males are favored of the Lord because they are ordained to hold the priesthood. Anyone who believes that does not understand the great plan of happiness. The premortal and mortal natures of men and women were specified by the Lord Jehovah Himself, and it is simply not within His character to diminish the roles and responsibilities of any of His children.

As President Joseph Fielding Smith explained: "The Lord offers to his daughters every spiritual gift and blessing that can be obtained by his sons" ("Magnifying Our Callings in the Priesthood," *Improvement Era,* June 1970, 66). We know that all of us, men and women alike, receive the gift of the Holy Ghost and are entitled to personal revelation. We may all take upon us the Lord's name, become the sons and daughters of Christ, partake of the ordinances of the temple from which we emerge endowed with power, receive the fulness of the gospel, and achieve exaltation in the celestial kingdom. These spiritual blessings are available to men and women alike, according to their faithfulness and their efforts to receive them.

The basic doctrinal purpose for the creation of the earth is to provide for God's spirit children the continuation of the process of exaltation and eternal life. God said to Moses, "And I, God, created man in mine own image, in the image of mine Only Begotten created I him; male and female created I them. And I, God, blessed them, and said unto them: Be fruitful, and multiply, and replenish the earth" (Moses 2:27–28).

This doctrine sometimes causes women to ask: "Is a woman's value dependent exclusively upon her role as a wife and mother?" The answer is simple and obvious—no! Motherhood and marital status are not the only measures of a woman's worth. Some women do not have the privilege of marrying or rearing children in this life. To the worthy, these blessings will come later. Women who do have the privilege of rearing children will, of course, be held accountable for that priceless, eternal stewardship. While there is simply not a more significant contribution you can make to society, to the Church, or to the eternal destiny of our Father's children than what you do as a mother, motherhood is not the only measure of goodness or of one's acceptance before the Lord. Every righteous woman has a significant role to play in the onward march of the kingdom of God.

I have a deep and abiding feeling about women and about the crucial role they play in every important setting, particularly in the family and in the Church. I have spoken boldly about the role women must play in the councils of the Church. We cannot fulfill our mission as a Church without the inspired insight and support of women.

For that reason I am concerned about what I see happening with some of our young women and

some of our not-so-young women. The adversary is having a heyday distorting attitudes about gender and roles and families and individual worth. He is the author of mass confusion about values and roles, the contribution and the unique nature of women. Today's popular culture, which is preached by every form of media from the silver screen to the Internet, celebrates the sexy, saucy, socially aggressive woman. These distortions are seeping into the thinking of some of our own women in the Church.

My deep desire is to clarify how we in the presiding councils of the Church feel about the sisters of this Church, how our Heavenly Father feels about His daughters, and what He expects of them. My dear sisters, we believe in you.

We believe in and are counting on your goodness and your strength, your propensity for virtue and valor, your kindness and courage, your skill and resilience. We believe in your mission as women of God. We realize that you are the emotional (and sometimes spiritual) glue that holds families and often ward families together. We believe that the Church simply will not accomplish what it must without your faith and faithfulness, your innate tendency to put the well-being of others ahead of your own, and your spiritual strength and tenacity.

Regardless of the variety of situations in which women live, where the women are righteous and good, love, peace, and joy abound in the home. When children are in the home, every effort should be made by mothers to be home for them. All righteous women are part of God's great plan for His daughters to become queens and to receive the highest blessings in time or eternity.

On the other hand, Satan's plan is to get you so preoccupied with the world's glitzy lies about women that you completely miss what you have come here to do and to become. Remember, he wants us to "be miserable like unto himself" (2 Nephi 2:27). Never lose your precious identity by doing anything that would jeopardize the promised eternal future your Heavenly Father has provided for you.

Women have labored valiantly in the cause of truth and righteousness from before the foundations of the world. In President Joseph F. Smith's vision of the redemption of the dead, he saw not only Father Adam and other prophets but "our glorious Mother Eve, with many of her faithful daughters who had lived through the ages and worshiped the true and living God" (D&C 138:39).

Think about the incomparable role of Eve, whose actions set in motion the great plan of our Father, and about Mary, the "precious and chosen vessel" (Alma 7:10) who bore the Christ Child.

Surely no one would question the contribution made by those majestic women.

Our dispensation is not without its heroines. Countless women from every continent and walk of life have made dramatic contributions to the cause of Christ. Consider Lucy Mack Smith, the mother of the martyred Prophet Joseph and Hyrum and the grandmother of President Joseph F. Smith. Her resilience and righteousness under the most emotionally and spiritually taxing conditions surely influenced her prophet sons and set them firmly on the path towards fulfilling their foreordained destiny.

At this point you may be thinking, "But what about me and my contribution? I'm not Eve or Mary or even Lucy Mack Smith. I'm just regular, plain old me. Is there something about my contribution that is significant to the Lord? Does He really need me?" Remember, the righteous who are

not highly visible are valued too and, in the words of a Book of Mormon prophet, are "no less serviceable unto the people" (Alma 48:19).

President Spencer W. Kimball responded to that question this way: "Both a righteous man and a righteous woman are a blessing to all those whom their lives touch.

" . . . [In] the world before we came here, faithful women were given certain assignments while faithful men were foreordained to certain priesthood tasks. While we do not now remember the particulars, . . . [we] are accountable for those things which long ago were expected of us" (*My Beloved Sisters* [Deseret Book, 1979], 37).

Every sister in this Church who has made covenants with the Lord has a divine mandate to help save souls, to lead the women of the world, to strengthen the homes of Zion, and to build the kingdom of God. Sister Eliza R. Snow, the second general president of the Relief Society, said: "Every sister in this church should be a preacher of righteousness . . . because we have greater and higher privileges than any other females upon the face of the earth." ("Great Indignation Meeting," *Deseret Evening News,* 14 January 1870, 2).

Every sister who stands for truth and righteousness diminishes the influence of evil. Dear sisters, every one of you who strengthens and protects your family is doing the work of God. Every sister who lives as a woman of God becomes a beacon for others to follow and plants seeds of righteous influence that will be harvested for decades to come. Every sister who makes and keeps sacred covenants becomes an instrument in the hands of God.

I have been drawn to an interchange between God the Father and His Eldest and Only Begotten Son, who is the ultimate example of living up to one's premortal promises. When God asked who would come to earth to prepare a way for all mankind to be saved and strengthened and blessed, it was Jesus Christ who said, simply, "Here am I, send me" (Abraham 3:27).

Just as the Savior stepped forward to fulfill His divine responsibilities, we have the challenge and responsibility to do likewise. If you are wondering if you make a difference to the Lord, imagine the effect when you make such commitments as the following:

"Father, if you need a woman to rear children in righteousness, Here am I, send me."

"If you need a woman to make a house a home filled with love, Here am I, send me."

"If you need a woman who will shun vulgarity and dress modestly and speak with dignity and show the world how joyous it is to keep the commandments, Here am I, send me."

"If you need a woman who can resist the

alluring temptations of the world by keeping her eyes fixed on eternity, Here am I, send me."

Between now and the day the Lord comes again, He needs women in every family, in every ward, in every community, in every nation who will step forward in righteousness and say by their words and their actions, "Here am I, send me."

My question is, Will you be one of those women?

Now, I know you want to. But how will you do it? How, in a world filled with deceptive messages about women and the family, and knowing the significance of both to the Lord, will you perpetually respond to the Lord by saying, "Here am I, send me"?

For those who really want to live up to who you are, for those who at all costs want to repent, if necessary, and who want to see through Satan's deceptions, may I suggest that you listen to and

follow those whom you sustain as prophets, seers, and revelators. I suggest that you learn to hear the voice of the Spirit, or the voice of the Lord as communicated by the power of the Holy Ghost.

I cannot stress enough the importance of listening to and following the prophet and the Apostles. In today's world, where twenty-four hours a day the media's talking heads spew forth conflicting opinions, where men and women jockey for everything from your money to your vote, there is one unpolluted, unbiased, clear voice that you can always count on. And that is the voice of the living prophet and the Apostles. Our only motive is "the everlasting welfare of your souls" (2 Nephi 2:30).

Think of it! Think about the value of having a source of information that you can always count on, that will always have your eternal interests at heart, and that will always provide inspired truth. That's a phenomenal gift and guide.

If you want to avoid the snares of Satan, if you need direction when the choices in front of you are puzzling and perplexing, learn to hear the voice of the Lord as communicated through the Holy Ghost. And then, of course, do what it tells you to do.

Nephi taught clearly that the Holy Ghost is the "gift of God unto all those who diligently seek him" and that "he that diligently seeketh shall find" (1 Nephi 10:17, 19). The unquestionable reality is that you control how close you are to the Lord. You determine just how clear and readily available promptings from the Holy Ghost will be. You determine this by your actions, by your attitude, by the choices you make, by the things you watch and wear and listen to and read, and by how consistently and sincerely you invite the Spirit into your life.

As life progresses, how will you respond to

challenges that will inevitably come? Will you know where to turn for peace and consolation if your marriage faces hard times or health challenges loom up or you are called upon to bury a child—as two of our own children have done—or if a child threatens to stray from the gospel path? How will you know what to do when you face financial reverses? Where will you turn for insight and inspiration when you are called upon to lead in your ward or stake? You dear mothers, where will you turn for strength to care for and lead your family on Sundays when your husbands are serving as priesthood leaders in your stake or ward?

There is only one way to safely and confidently meet the obstacles and opportunities that are part of life's path: Listen to the prophet and the Apostles, study the principles we teach, and then take those principles to the Lord and ask Him how you should apply them in your life. Ask Him to influence your thoughts, temper your actions, and guide your steps. "Counsel with the Lord in all thy doings, and he will direct thee for good" (Alma 37:37). He will communicate with you through the power and the presence of the Holy Ghost.

There are several things you can do to greatly enhance your ability to understand the promptings of the Holy Ghost and thereby hear and respond to the voice of God. Let me tell you what they are.

First, fast and pray. When the sons of Mosiah were united with Alma the Younger, they rejoiced in their reunion and acknowledged that because "they had given themselves to much prayer, and fasting" they had been given the spirit of prophecy and revelation, "and when they taught, they taught with power and authority of God" (Alma 17:3).

Second, immerse yourself in the scriptures. The word of God will "tell you all things what ye should do" (2 Nephi 32:3). The scriptures are a conduit for personal revelation. I urge you to intensify your study of them. I promise that your ability to hear the voice of the Lord as communicated through the Holy Ghost will increase and improve.

Third, prepare to spend time in the house of the Lord. When the appropriate time comes for you to go to the temple, you will leave the temple "armed with . . . power" (D&C 109:22) and with the promise that as you "grow up" in your knowledge of the Lord you will "receive a fulness of the Holy Ghost" (D&C 109:15). The temple is a place of personal revelation. If you are endowed, visit the temple regularly. If you are not, prepare yourself to enter. Inside the doors of the temple rests the power that will fortify you against the vicissitudes of life.

Fourth, listen to the counsel of your parents and your husband. They are usually wise and experienced. Share with them your fears and concerns. Seek blessings from your father or your husband. If he has gone to the other side of the veil, or if for some reason he is not worthy or able, go to your bishop or your stake president. They love you and will count it a privilege to bless your life. If you haven't yet done so, you should also receive your patriarchal blessing.

Fifth, practice obedience and repentance. There are certain things you simply cannot do if you want to have the Holy Ghost with you. It is not possible to listen to inappropriate music, watch movies or soap operas filled with sexual innuendo, tamper with pornography on the Internet (or anywhere else for that matter), take the name of the Lord in vain, wear revealing clothing, or compromise in any way the law of chastity. Mothers, you particularly must set the example of modesty in dress and action. You cannot disregard the values of true womanhood and expect the Holy Ghost to remain with you. Whenever anyone participates in those kinds of activities, it should not be a surprise that feelings of loneliness, discouragement, and unworthiness follow. Do not make the choice to go it alone rather than have the Spirit of the Lord to guide, to protect, to prompt, to warn, and to fill you with peace. Repent if you need to so you can enjoy the companionship of the Spirit.

Women and men who can hear the voice of the Lord and who respond to those promptings become invaluable instruments in His hands.

Finally, my dear sisters, you have a profound, innate spiritual ability to hear the voice of the Good Shepherd. You need never wonder again if you have worth in the sight of the Lord and to the Brethren in the presiding councils of the Church. We love you. We cherish you. We respect you. Never doubt that your influence is absolutely vital to preserving the family and to assisting with the growth and spiritual vitality of the Church. This Church will not reach its foreordained destiny without you. We men simply cannot nurture as you nurture. Most of us don't have the sensitivity, spiritual and otherwise, that by your eternal nature you inherently have. Your influence on families and with children, youth, and men is singular. You are natural-born nurturers. Because of these unusual gifts and talents, you are vital to taking the gospel to all the world, to demonstrating that there is joy in living the way prophets have counseled us to live. I encourage you to never, never stop teaching, and never allow your wisdom of a lifetime of faithful dedication to the Lord to grow dim in your own families or your wards.

Today more than ever, we need women of faith, virtue, vision, and charity, as the Relief Society Declaration proclaims. We need women who can hear and will respond to the voice of the Lord, women who at all costs will defend and protect the family. We don't need women who want to be like men, sound like men, dress like men, drive like some men, or act like men. We do need women who rejoice in their womanhood and have a spiritual confirmation of their identity, their value, and their eternal destiny. Above all, we need women who will stand up for truth and righteousness and decry evil at every turn, women who will simply say, "Here am I, Lord, send me."